Operation Order!

Fun practise erations

John Enock

Introduction	3
Chapter 1: Getting Started	5
Does Order Matter?	5
Exercises 1 and 2	5
When does the order matter?	6
Exercises 3 and 4	6
Chapter 2: The Order of Operations	7
The Order of Operations	7
Exercise 5	8
Chapter 3: Brackets	9
Exercise 6	9
Exercise 7 - Target Number Challenges	10
Exercise 8	10
Chapter 4: Powers and Roots	11
Brackets	11
Exercise 9	12
Chapter 5: Putting it all Together	13
Exercise 10	13
Using BIDMAS	14
Exercises 11 and 12	14
Chapter 6: Puzzles	15
Excercise 13	15
Boxes 1-5	15
Boxes 6-8	16
Boxes 9-10	17
Boxes 11-12	18
The 24 Game	19
Exercise 14	20
Quaso Puzzles	21
Answers	25

ALSO AVAILABLE FROM JOHN ENOCK FOR GIFTED STUDENTS:
Cryptic Cross Numbers
ISBN 978 1 90755 021 8

Operation Order!
© John Enock 2015

Book   ISBN 978 1 911093 04 6
Ebook ISBN 978 1 911093 05 3

Tarquin,   Distributed in the USA by Parkwest
Suite 74 Holywell Hill   www.parkwestpubs.com
St Albans AL1 1DT   www.amazon.com & major retailers
UK

www.tarquingroup.com   Distributed in Australia by OLM www.lat-olm.com.au

Photocopying is authorised within a single purchasing institution.
Photocopying is not authorised outside the purchasing organisation, nor can the material be held in any electronic database or be distributed electronically without the permission of the Publisher.

A catalogue record for this book is available from the British Library.

Printed in the UK, Australia and USA.

Introduction

The intention of this book is threefold:

1) To explain and make clear the order in which arithmetical operations take place through the aid of worked examples, questions and puzzles
2) To dispel any myths, misconceptions and misunderstandings concerning the order of operations
3) To foster an enjoyment of problem and puzzle solving involving order of operations.

The book is divided into 6 chapters. Key concepts are introduced, explained and enlarged upon in the first five together with a number of topic-related puzzles in the final chapter. The book will also hopefully reinforce essential computational skills such as mental arithmetic, use of brackets and indices, decimals, problem-solving and logical thinking.

Teachers may find many of the activities useful as a lesson 'starter' where ideas can be presented, discussed and questioned with students who will then be in a position to tackle the exercises themselves. In the case of the puzzle activities in particular, it is strongly recommended that examples are demonstrated on a Smartboard, with students making active contributions as the activity progresses. Some students may not get as far as the Quaso puzzles, though it is to be hoped that they will appeal to the student (and teacher!) who enjoys grid number puzzles of this type. It is not necessary for a calculator to be used in any of the examples, though of course they can be used for verification of answers. This in itself should provide a fruitful source for discussion as clearly it will sometimes be the case that the two answers thus obtained will not match up!

The book is not intended to be a textbook, but as a resource for numeracy enrichment. Students who are already in possession of a sound understanding of the principles of order of operations may simply enjoy the problem-solving exercises and puzzles rather than working through the exercises in the first few chapters. The book is therefore a flexible resource in terms of pupil attainment and age range and is probably best suited to students aged between 10 and 14, overlapping both Key Stages 2 and 3.

Chapter 1: Getting Started

Does Order Matter?

Exercise 1

Work out these sums

1. a) 4 + 3 = ☐   b) 3 + 4 = ☐
2. a) 3 + 4 + 5 = ☐   b) 4 + 3 + 5 = ☐   c) 5 + 3 + 4 = ☐
3. a) 1 + 3 + 5 + 7 = ☐   b) 3 + 1 + 7 + 5 = ☐
4. a) 2 + 4 + 3 + 9 + 6 = ☐   b) 4 + 9 + 2 + 6 + 3 = ☐
5. a) 42 + 38 = ☐   b) 38 + 42 = ☐

 What do you notice?

Exercise 2

Now try these

1. a) 3 × 4 = ☐   b) 4 × 3 = ☐
2. a) 2 × 3 × 5 = ☐   b) 3 × 5 × 2 = ☐
3. a) 12 × 6 = ☐   b) 6 × 12 = ☐
4. a) 13 × 4 = ☐   b) 4 × 13 = ☐
5. a) 2 × 3 × 5 × 7 = ☐   b) 3 × 5 × 7 × 2 = ☐

 What do you notice this time?

When Does the Order Matter?

It looks like the *order* of the numbers doesn't seem to matter.

Is this always true?

Consider 8 – 5 and 5 – 8

Are the answers the same?

Now look at 12 ÷ 3 and 3 ÷ 12

Are they the same?

It looks like the **order** that numbers are written **does** matter.
It doesn't seem to matter with Addition and Multiplication but it does for Subtraction and Division.

Exercise 3
Try these, working left to right
Use a calculator once you have finished to check your answers

1.	a) 8 + 3 – 5 = ☐	b) 8 – 5 + 3 = ☐
2.	a) 10 – 3 + 1 – 4 = ☐	b) 10 – 4 + 1 – 3 = ☐
3.	a) 5 + 7 – 1 + 2 – 3 = ☐	b) 5 – 3 + 2 – 1 + 7 = ☐

You should get the same answer in each part.
This means that we can change the order of the numbers to get the same answer but the **sign** of the number must go with it.

Exercise 4

4.	a) 7 + 3 – 5 = ☐	b) 7 + 5 – 3 = ☐
5.	a) 6 – 1 + 4 – 3 = ☐	b) 4 + 1 + 3 – 6 = ☐
6.	a) 2 + 5 – 1 – 3 + 6 = ☐	b) 6 – 2 + 1 – 3 + 5 = ☐

You should get different numbers for a) and b)

Why?

Chapter 2: The Order of Operations

The Order of Operations

Now we are going to look at the *order* in which *operations* are done. *Operations* are what we *do* with numbers and include:

- Addition
- Subtraction
- Multiplication
- Division

(There are other Operations too – like using brackets and indices which we will come to later.)
Let's try *mixing* the operations up a bit more. We'll start with addition and multiplication.

$5 \times 4 + 3$ is obviously equal to 23

There is a special order that operations are done in. You might think the answer to
$3 + 4 \times 5$ is 35 – but it isn't.
Multiplication is more "important" than addition, Multiplication "takes precedence" over addition.
In fact $3 + 4 \times 5 = 23$.

Can you now see why?

This is true of division as well. Both × and ÷ *take precedence* over + and –
You can remember it like this

M	A
D	S

Practising the Order of Operations

Remember!

```
M  A
D  S
```

× and ÷ count the same e.g.
$$12 ÷ 6 × 3 = 12 × 6 ÷ 3$$

Here are some examples with answers to help you.

1. $4 + 2 × 3$ = 10
2. $5 + 8 ÷ 4$ = 7
3. $10 - 2 × 4$ = 2
4. $20 - 12 ÷ 3$ = 16
5. $8 × 2 + 3 × 4$ = 28

Exercise 5

1. $6 + 2 × 3$ =
2. $3 + 6 ÷ 2$ =
3. $10 - 3 × 3$ =
4. $12 - 8 ÷ 4$ =
5. $4 + 4 × 4$ =
6. $2 × 5 + 3 × 4$ =
7. $6 × 3 - 2 × 5$ =
8. $4 × 8 + 15 ÷ 3$ =
9. $24 ÷ 3 - 2 × 4$ =
10. $2 + 3 × 5 + 9$ =

Chapter 3: Brackets

Brackets

If we put brackets around two or more numbers then this calculation is done first

$(5 + 3) \times 4 = 32$

The 5 and 3 are added together *first*.
Brackets *take precedence* over **all** other operations.
Sometimes the × sign is left out when a number is placed *just before* a bracket – so:

$4(3 + 5)$ means $4 \times (3 + 5)$

- Be careful with calculations like this:
  $6 + 3(2+5)$
- Do the sum inside the brackets first
- Then multiply by 3
- Then add 6

$$6 + 3(2 + 5)$$
$$= 6 + 3 \times 7$$
$$= 6 + 21$$
$$= 27$$

Exercise 6

1. $4(3 + 5)$ = ☐
2. $(3 + 3) \times 7$ = ☐
3. $3(2 + 5) - 9$ = ☐
4. $(7 - 3) \times 8$ = ☐
5. $9(5 - 2) + 3$ = ☐
6. $(3 + 4) \times (7 - 2)$ = ☐
7. $(9 - 2) \times (9 - 3)$ = ☐
8. $(16 - 1) \div (8 - 5)$ = ☐
9. $1 + 3(4 + 6)$ = ☐
10. $20 - 2(3 + 7)$ = ☐
11. $3(7 - 2) + 5(9 - 4)$ = ☐
12. $2(5 + 6) + 3(2 + 8)$ = ☐

Target Number Challenges

Put in +, -, ×, ÷ or brackets to make the following sums correct. The first three have been done for you – work out how they have been done and then try the rest.

Exercise 7

1. 3 (4 + 2)			=	18		9. 8	3	4	=	20	(Two answers)
2. 3 + 4 - 2			=	5		8	3	4	=	20	
3. 3 × 4 + 2			=	14		10. 9	6	2	=	5	
4. 5	6	4	=	34		11. 2	3	4	5	=	24
5. 5	6	4	=	29		12. 2	3	4	5	=	26
6. 10	2	3	=	5		13. 2	3	4	5	=	19
7. 10	2	3	=	4		14. 2	3	4	5	=	15
8. 8	3	4	=	6		15. 2	3	4	5	=	6

What other numbers can you make using 2,3,4,5 *without* changing the order?

Exercise 8 – Ten More!

1. 8	4	3	6	=	10		6. 3	4	6	8	= 35
2. 8	4	3	6	=	14		7. 8	2	6	3	= 6
3. 8	4	3	6	=	13		8. 8	2	6	3	= 26
4. 8	4	3	6	=	50		9. 9	3	5	7	= 45
5. 3	4	6	8	=	16		10. 9	3	5	7	= 17

Chapter 4: Powers and Roots

Indices

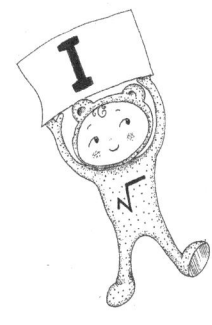

Nearly There!
- You may know that 3^2 means $3 \times 3 = 9$. The little "2" is called an index. **Indices** is the **plural** of index. Another word for index is **exponent**, or **power**.
- Calculations involving indices are done **after** brackets, but **before** the other operations. Indices **take precedence** over addition, subtraction, multiplication and division.
- Let's see how it works:

(i) 3×5^2	(ii) $20 - 4^2$	(iii) $2^3 + 3^2$
$= 3 \times 5 \times 5$ (Do the 5^2 **first**)	$= 20 - 4 \times 4$	$= 8 + 9$
$= \mathbf{75}$	$= 20 - 16$	$= \mathbf{17}$
	$= \mathbf{4}$	

Roots

You may remember things like

$\sqrt{9} = 3$	$\sqrt{64} = 8$	and so on

A **root** is treated in the same way as an **index**, and, in fact, can be thought of as a *type of index*.

*Research project: find out how roots are represented as indices. Present your findings to the class. Impress your teacher!

Examples

(i) $4 \times \sqrt{9}$ (can be written $4\sqrt{9}$)

$= 4 \times 3$

$= 12$

(ii) $3^2 \times \sqrt{16}$

$= 9 \times 4$

$= 36$

Exercise 9

1) $5 + 3 - 1 - 6$ =

2) $5 + 12 \div 3$ =

3) $3(2 + 7)$ =

4) $4^2 - 2 \times 8$ =

5) $4 \times 5 - 3^2$ =

6) $6 \div 3 \times 4$ =

7) $30 - 16 \div 2$ =

8) $(4 + 3)^2$ =

9) $\sqrt{(4 \times 9)}$ =

10) $6^2 \div \sqrt{4}$ =

Chapter 5

Putting it All Together

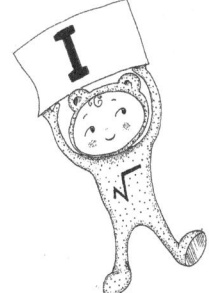

We have a total of **six** operations
- Brackets
- Indices
- Multiplication and Division
- Addition and Subtraction

It might help you to remember the **order** of operations by visualising

BIDAMS

*Note: This is sometimes known as

BODMAS

because the 'O' is used for the word 'Order', instead of 'I' for indices. Bit confusing, I know.

Many of you will have come across BIDMAS before, but when it is written out like this it gives a wrong impression of the order of operations. For instance you might think think that addition is more important than subtraction, which it isn't.

The answer to a sum like 12 - 3 + 4 is 13. If you thought the answer was 5, it is because you added the 3 and 4 together first, which is incorrect! Addition and subtraction have equal 'weight'.

Exercise 10

1) $2^3 + 3^2$ =
2) $2^3 \times 3^2$ =
3) $20 - 2^4$ =
4) $\sqrt{9} \times \sqrt{4}$ =
5) $(8 - 3)^2$ =
6) $3(1 + 4^2)$ =
7) $3^2(1 + 3^2)$ =
8) $\sqrt{(3^2 + 4^2)}$ =
9) $50 \div 5^2$ =
10) $100 - 4(3^2 - 1)$ =

Using BIDMAS

- Occasionally it is not clear how to use BIDMAS

- This is a very common type of calculation

$$\frac{7.2 - 1.6}{1.2 - 0.5}$$

Even with a calculator it's easy to do this wrong!

- It must be done by working out the top of the fraction (the numerator) **separately** to the bottom (the denominator).

$$\text{Top} \quad 7.2 - 1.6 = 5.6$$
$$\text{Bottom} \quad 1.2 - 0.5 = 0.7$$

$$\frac{\text{Top}}{\text{Bottom}} = \frac{5.6}{0.7} = 8$$

- The whole calculation really means

$$(7.2 - 1.6) \div (1.2 - 0.5)$$

and this is probably the best way of working it out using a calculator.

- The answers to the following questions are all **whole numbers**
- Use a calculator for each question

Exercise 11

1) $\dfrac{4.8 \times 7.5}{4.8 + 4.2} = \square$

2) $\dfrac{7.2 \div 0.4}{2 \times 3^2} = \square$

3) $\dfrac{2 \times 3 + 4 \times 5}{1.3 \times 0.5} = \square$

4) $\dfrac{8^2 - 7^2}{3^2 - 2^2} = \square$

5) $1 + \dfrac{1}{2}\left(\dfrac{12}{1.5 \times 4}\right) = \square$

Exercise 12

Fill in the boxes with the numbers given to make the calculations correct

1) $\square + \square \div \square = 9$ (4,7,8)	6) $\square + \square \times (\square + \square) = 34$ (3,4,5,7)
2) $\square - \square \times \square = 2$ (2,3,8)	7) $\square \times (\square - \square - \square) = 48$ (1,2,8,9)
3) $\square \div \square \times \square = 14$ (3,6,7)	8) $\square \times (\square + \square) + \square = 37$ (2,3,6,7)
4) $\square \times \square + \square \times \square = 22$ (2,3,4,5)	*9) $\square \times \square - \square \wedge \square = 1$ (1,2,3,9)
5) $\square - \square \times \square + \square = 8$ (2,4,7,9)	*10) $\square \wedge \square - \square \wedge \square = 39$ (2,3,4,5)

*The ^ symbol means "to the power of"

Chapter 6: Puzzles

Boxes

Fill in the numbers 1, 2, 3, 4 (using each only once) in the empty boxes to make the totals given outside each box.

Exercise 13

1)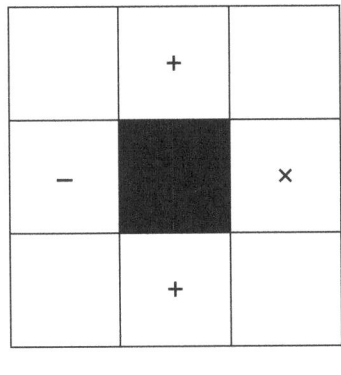

3)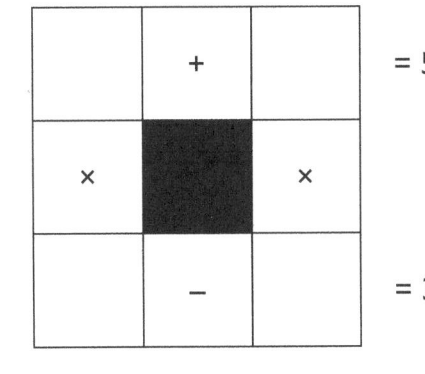

2)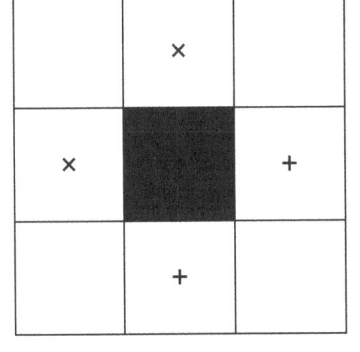

4)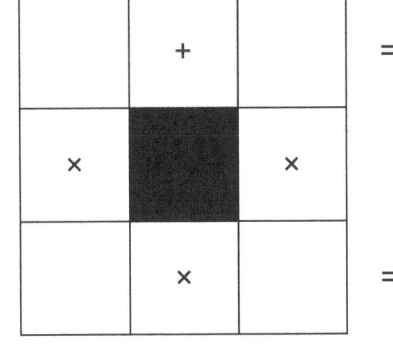

In questions 5-8, use the numbers 1, 2, 3, 4, 5, 6. Use each number **once only**

5)

6)

	+		÷		= 8
+	■	×	■	−	
	×		−		= 11
= 9		= 18		= 1	

7)

	×		−		= 19
−	■	×	■	+	
	+		×		= 15
= 1		= 30		= 3	

8)

	×		÷		= 10
−	■	÷	■	+	
	×		×		= 8
= 4		= 3		= 7	

The last four are more difficult. Use the numbers 1, 2, 3, 4, 5, 6, 7, 8, 9. Remember to use each number only **once**.

9)

	×		×		= 24
+	▓	×	▓	+	
	+		×		= 47
+	▓	−	▓	+	
	+		×		= 73
= 10		= 13		= 17	

10)

	−		÷		= 1
+	▓	+	▓	+	
	×		×		= 28
+	▓	+	▓	×	
	−		÷		= 3
= 15		= 24		= 5	

17

Use the numbers 1, 2, 3, 4, 5, 6, 7, 8, 9. Remember to use each number only **once**.

11)

	+		×		= 22
+	■	−	■	+	
	−		÷		= 5
×	■	÷	■	×	
	+		×		= 26

= 55   = 5   = 13

12)

	+		+		= 21
−	■	+	■	−	
	+		×		= 19
×	■	÷	■	−	
	+		+		= 12

= 2   = 11   = 0

The 24 Game

A Game for 2 Players

- You will need a pack of cards with all the tens, jacks, queens and kings taken out.

How to Play

- Shuffle and deal four cards
- The object of the game is to make a total of 24 with the four cards by inserting $+, -, \times, \div$ or brackets. You can include indices and square roots if you like!
- Both you and your partner have a go at making the total **without** rearranging the cards.
- The first player to correctly make the total gains 10 points.
- If neither of you can manage this, then you can re-arrange the numbers. You earn 5 points if you can reach the target of 24.

Examples

Game 1

- Player A deals

$$2, 5, 6, 8$$

- Player B claims 10 points by making

$$2 \times 5 + 6 + 8 = 24$$

Game 2

- Player B deals

$$3, 7, 1, 3$$

- Player A says

$$3 \times 7 + 1 \times 3 = 24$$

player A wins 10 points

Game 3

- The cards dealt are

$$2, 9, 1, 7$$

- Neither player can see how to make 24, but player A wins 5 points by going like this

$$7 \times \sqrt{9} + 2 + 1$$

- The first to 50 points wins.
- Challenge your teacher to a game!
- Here are some 24 challenges for you to try. You can put the numbers in a different order if you wish. The first two have been done for you.

Exercise 14

1)	2 5 5 9	5 (5 – 2) + 9
2)	2 5 8 9	(8 – 2) × (9 – 5)
3)	2 2 3 9	
4)	1 3 3 3	
5)	4 4 4 4	
6)	1 2 5 7	
7)	5 5 7 7	
8)	3 3 8 9	
9)	2 2 3 8	

Quaso Puzzles

- Here is another puzzle called **Quaso**. It is a bit like the '24' game but the target number is different each time. The target number is stated next to each puzzle. Try to fill in the blank squares to make the target number. The operations are already given.
- An index is represented by ^ which reads "to the power of".
- The first two puzzles are given with the answers so that you can see what is going on.
- Notice that **all the answers are different**. This is true in every puzzle.
- And each digit must be used once only in each answer.
- A diamond symbol represents one of the digits at the top of the puzzle.
- Two diamonds close together represents a two digit number.
- The capital letters A and B denote the **across** answers (those horizontal, or in the rows).
- a and b are the **down** answers (those vertical, or in the columns).

Quaso No 1
Target Number: 11
Digits used: 1,2,4,5

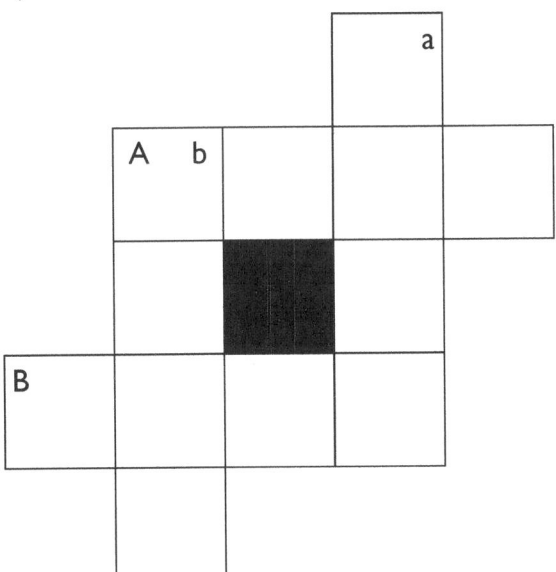

A) ◇ ^ ◇ − ◇ × ◇
B) ◇◇ − ◇ + ◇

a) ◇◇ − ◇ − √◇
b) ◇(◇ − ◇) − ◇

21

Solving Quaso Puzzles
- The target number is stated next to each puzzle. Try to fill in the blank squares to make the target number. The operations are already given.
- An index is represented by ^ which reads "to the power of"
- All the answers are different and each digit must be used once only in each answer
- A diamond symbol represents one of the digits at the top of the puzzle
- Two diamonds close together represents a two digit number
- The capital letters A and B denote the across answers - a and b are the down answers

Quaso No 2
Target Number: 30
Digits used: 1, 2, 6, 8

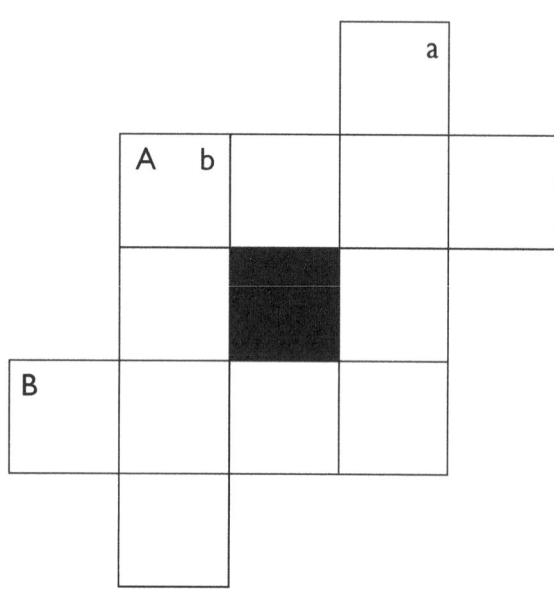

A) ◇ × √◇◇ − ◇
B) (◇ − ◇)(◇ − ◇)

a) ◇(◇ + ◇ + ◇)
b) ◇(◇ + ◇) + ◇

Quaso No 3
Target Number: 19
Digits used: 1, 4, 6, 9

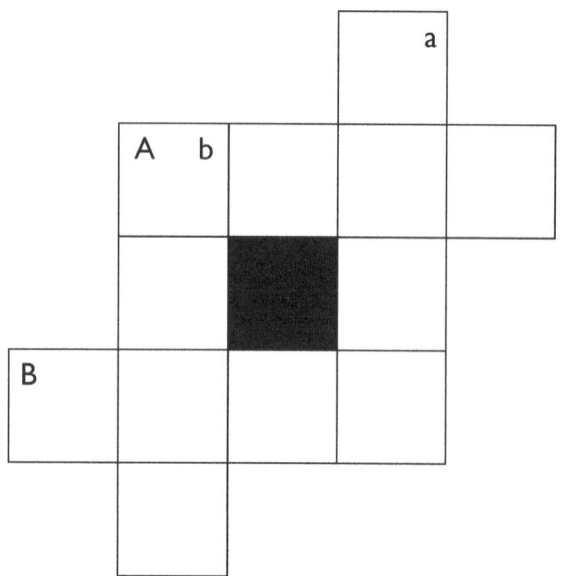

A) ◇ × √◇ + ◇ + ◇
B) ◇(◇ − ◇) + ◇

a) ◇ + ◇ + ◇ × ◇
b) ◇(◇ + ◇) − ◇

Solving Quaso Puzzles
- The target number is stated next to each puzzle. Try to fill in the blank squares to make the target number. The operations are already given.
- An index is represented by ^ which reads "to the power of"
- All the answers are different and each digit must be used once only in each answer
- A diamond symbol represents one of the digits at the top of the puzzle
- Two diamonds close together represents a two digit number
- The capital letters A and B denote the across answers - a and b are the down answers

Quaso No 4
Target Number: 15
Digits used: 2, 3, 4, 5

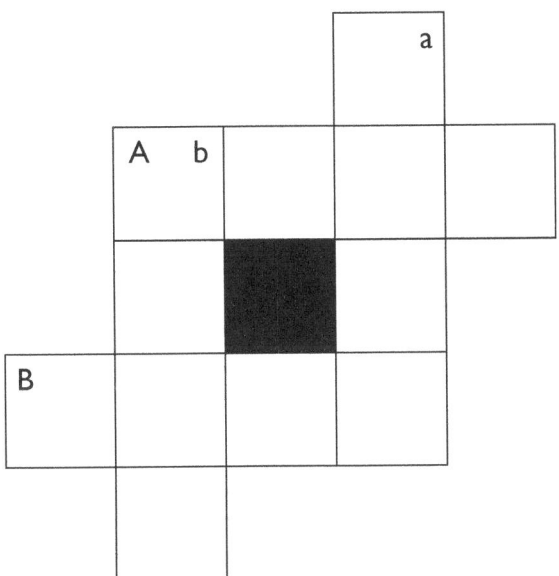

A) $\diamond(\diamond - \diamond) + \diamond$
B) $\diamond \wedge \diamond + \diamond + \sqrt{\diamond}$

a) $\diamond \times \diamond + \diamond + \diamond$
b) $\diamond(\diamond + \diamond) - \diamond$

Quaso No 5
Target Number: 21
Digits used: 2, 3, 5, 6

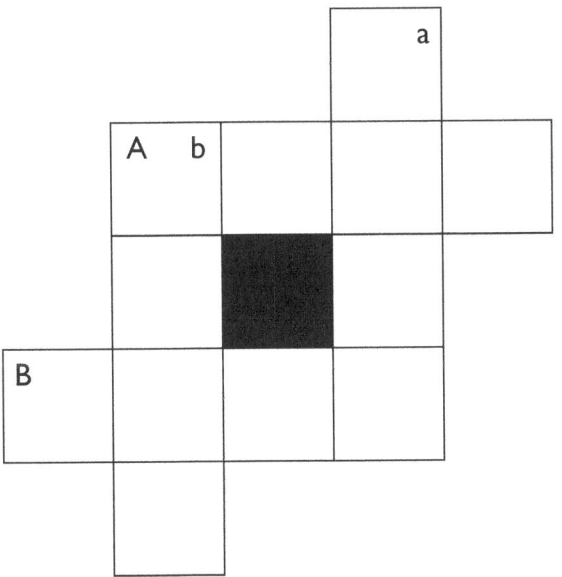

A) $\diamond \times \diamond + \diamond - \diamond$
B) $(\diamond + \diamond)(\diamond - \diamond)$

a) $\diamond(\diamond - \diamond) + \diamond$
b) $\diamond \times \sqrt{\diamond\diamond} + \diamond$

Solving Quaso Puzzles
- The target number is stated next to each puzzle. Try to fill in the blank squares to make the target number. The operations are already given.
- An index is represented by ^ which reads "to the power of"
- All the answers are different and each digit must be used once only in each answer
- A diamond symbol represents one of the digits at the top of the puzzle
- Two diamonds close together represents a two digit number
- The capital letters A and B denote the across answers - a and b are the down answers

Quaso No 6
Target Number: 27
Digits used: 2, 5, 6, 8

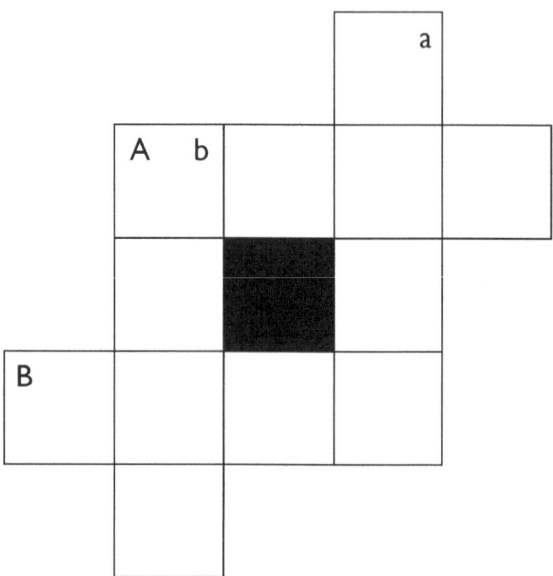

A) ◇(◇ − ◇) − ◇
B) ◇◇ + ◇ − ◇

a) ◇ ^ ◇ + ◇ − ◇
b) ◇ × ◇ + ◇ + ◇

Quaso No 7
Target Number: 33
Digits used: 3, 4, 6, 9

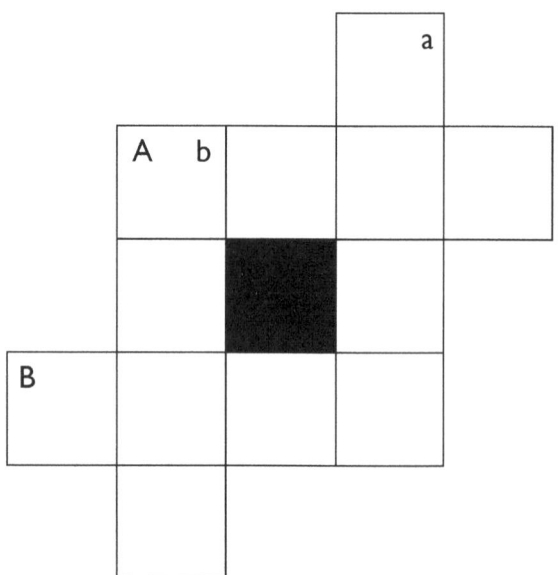

A) ◇ × ◇ + ◇ × √◇
B) ◇ × √◇◇ + ◇

a) ◇ × √◇◇ + ◇
b) ◇ × ◇ − ◇ + ◇

Answers

Chapter 1: Getting Started

Ex.1 Q.1a) 7   b) 7   Q.2a) 12   b) 12   c) 12   Q.3a) 16   b) 16   Q.4a) 24   b) 24   Q.5a) 80   b) 80

Ex.2 Q.1a) 12   b) 12   Q.2a) 30   b) 30   Q3.a) 72   b) 72   Q.4a) 52   b) 52   Q.5a) 210   b) 210

Ex.3 Q.1a) 6   b) 6   Q.2a) 4   b) 4   Q.3a) 10   b) 10

Ex.4 Q.4a) 5   b) 9   Q.5a) 6   b) 2   Q.6a) 9   b) 7

Chapter 2: Order of Operations

Ex.5 Q.1) 12   Q.2) 6   Q.3) 1   Q.4) 10   Q.5) 20   Q.6) 22   Q.7) 8   Q.8) 37   Q.9) 0   Q.10) 26

Chapter 3: Brackets

Ex.6 Q.1) 32   Q.2) 42   Q.3) 12   Q.4) 32   Q.5) 30   Q.6) 35
Q.7) 42   Q.8) 5   Q.9) 31   Q.10) 0   Q.11) 40   Q.12) 52

Ex.7 Q.4) 5 × 6 + 4   Q.5) 5 + 6 × 4
Q.6) 10 − 2 − 3 or 10 − (2 + 3)   Q.7) 10 − 2 × 3 or (10 + 2) ÷ 3
Q.8) 8 × 3 ÷ 4   Q.9) (8 − 3) × 4 or 8 × 3 − 4
Q.10) 9 − 6 + 2   Q.11) 2(3 + 4 + 5)
Q.12) 2 × 3 + 4 × 5   Q.13) 2(3 + 4) + 5 or 2 × 3 × 4 − 5
Q.14) 2 × 3 + 4 + 5 or (2 + 3) × 4 − 5 or -2 -3 + 4 × 5   Q.15) 2 + 3 − 4 + 5

Ex.8 Q.1) 8 ÷ 4 + 3 + 5 = 10   Q.2) 8 × 4 − 3 × 6 = 14
Q.3) 8 − 4 + 3 + 6 = 13   Q.4) 8(4 + 3) − 6 = 50
Q.5) 3 × 4 ÷ 6 × 8 = 16   Q.6) 3 + 4 × 6 + 8 = 35
Q.7) 8 ÷ 2 + 6 ÷ 3 = 6   Q.8) 8 + 2 (6 + 3) = 26
Q.9) 9 + 3(5 + 7) = 45   Q.10) 9 + 3 × 5 − 7 = 17

Chapter 4: Powers and Roots

Ex.9 Q.1) 1   Q.2) 9   Q.3) 27   Q.4) 0   Q.5) 11
Q.6) 8   Q.7) 22   Q.8) 49   Q.9) 6   Q.10) 18

Chapter 5: Putting It All Together

Ex.10   Q.1) 17   Q.2) 72   Q.3) 4   Q.4) 6   Q.5) 25
        Q.6) 51   Q.7) 90   Q.8) 5   Q.9) 2   Q.10) 68

Ex.11   Q.1) 4   Q.2) 1   Q.3) 40   Q.4) 3   Q.5) 2

Ex.12   Q.1) 7 + 8 ÷ 4   Q.2) 8 − 3 × 2   Q.3) 6 ÷ 3 × 7   Q.4) 3 × 4 + 2 × 5   Q.5) 9 − 2 × 4 + 7
        Q.6) 7 + 3(4 + 5)   Q.7) 8(9 − 2 − 1)   Q.8) 6(2 + 3) + 7   Q.9) 1 × 9 − 2 ^ 3   Q.10) 4 ^ 3 − 5 ^ 2

Chapter 6: Puzzles

[Boxes need to be completed digits as follows]

Ex. 13   Q.1)   4   2   Q.2)   2   1   Q.3)   3   2   Q.4)   1   3
                3   1   3   4   4   1   4   2

       Q.5)   5   2   1   Q.6)   5   6   2   Q.7)   4   5   1
                4   6   3   4   3   1   3   6   2

       Q.8)   5   6   3   Q.9)   4   3   2   Q.10)   5   8   2
                1   2   4   5   7   6   4   7   1
                                       1   8   9   6   9   3

       Q.11)   1   7   3   Q.12)   7   8   6
                 9   8   2   1   9   2
                 6   4   5   5   3   4

Ex. 14   Q.3) 2 × 3 + 2 × 9   or   2 × 2(9 − 3)   Q.4) 3 ^ 3 − 1 × 3   or   (1 + 3)(3 + 3)
         Q.5) 4 × 4 + 4 + 4   or   √4(4 + 4 + 4)   Q.6) 1 × 2(5 + 7)   or   5(7 − 2) − 1
         Q.7) (7 − 5)(7 + 5)   or   7 × 7 − 5 × 5   Q.8) 8(9 − 3 − 3)   or   8√9 × 3 ÷ 3
         Q.9) 2 × 3 × 8 ÷ 2   or   2 ^ 3 + 2 × 8   or   3 × 8 + 2 − 2   or   .....?
                               You may find some other solutions of your own.

Quaso Puzzles

Answers to Quaso Puzzles 1 and 2 are given with the puzzles.

Quaso No 3

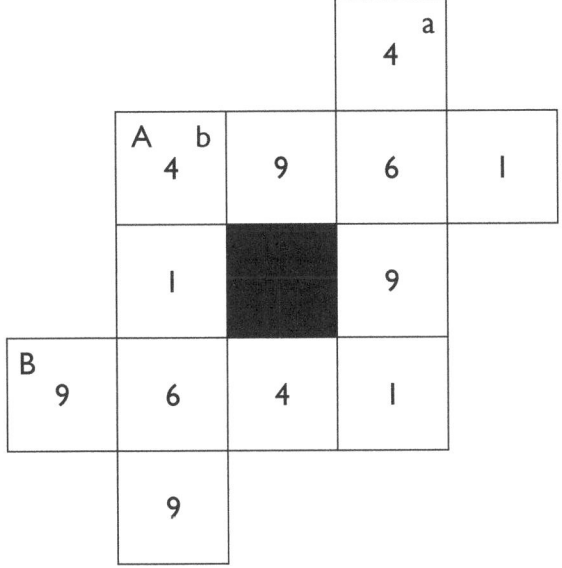

Quaso No 4

		3 a	
A b 4	5	2	3
2	■	5	
B 2	3	5	4
	5		

Quaso No 5

		6 a	
A b 3	6	5	2
2	■	2	
B 2	5	6	3
	6		

Quaso No 6

		5 a	
A b 8	6	2	5
2	■	8	
B 2	5	8	6
	6		

Quaso No 7

		4 a	
A b 4	6	3	9
9	■	6	
B 3	6	4	9
	3		

Tarquin Mathematics Resources

Tarquin has more than a thousand product lines to support and enrich mathematics. You can browse them at **www.tarquingroup.com**.

Recent titles include
ACE Mathematics Series
▶ Years 1-6: 6 books of games and activities
Without Words
▶ 2 books and 6 posters to promote mathematical thinking

Other Tarquin Products designed for you

Books

First Tables Colouring Book

Second Tables Colouring Book

Arithmetic Arithmetic

Tables Cubes

Mathematical Vocabulary 2

The Week's Problem

A Puzzle a Day

Junior Mathematical Team Games

Junior Mini Mathematical Murder Mysteries

Posters

One Million Poster

Multiples Poster

Equal Parts Poster

Quadrilaterals and Polygons Poster

Roman Numerals Poster

Dice and other Manipulatives

Excellent prices on 12-sided and 10-sided dice classroom packs — ideal for mental mathematics.

Tarquin, Suite 74, 17 Holywell Hill, St Albans, AL1 1DT
Tel: +44 (0)1727833866 Fax: +44 (0)845 456 6385
www.tarquingroup.com   Follow us on Twitter @TarquinGroup

Lightning Source UK Ltd.
Milton Keynes UK
UKOW07f0631151215

264745UK00004B/15/P